# *The Beautiful Unnamed*

A Zarigueya Press Book    Milwaukee, Wisconsin
Copyright 2015 © by Kathleen A Dale

All rights reserved under international and Pan-American Copyright Conventions. Published in the United States of America by Zarigueya Press, Milwaukee, Wisconsin.

Published by Zarigueya Press,
Milwaukee, Wisconsin
www.zarigueyapress.com

Library of Congress Cataloguing-in-Publication Data
Dale, Kathleen A
The Beautiful Unnamed
"A Zarigueya Press Book."
ISBN 9780972375436 (pbk.)

I.    Title
**First Edition**

**Cover Image**--Fractal, Public Domain
**Cover/Book Design and Layout**—Kathleen Dale

Printed in the United States of America

# The Beautiful Unnamed

poems by

**Kathleen A Dale**

Zarigueya Press, Milwaukee, WI
www.zarigueya.com

*for all my teachers, past and present*

# Table of Contents

Apophenia: An Apologia  5

**The Beautiful Unnamed**
    Quivira  9
    Chicken Dinner  16
    there is a wilderness  17
    A Child's Garden  18
    A Mother's Tale  20
    a stay  24
    The Beautiful Unnamed  25

**Family Snapshot**
    Family Snapshot  31
    Grounded  32
    Rose Sacrament  33
    Patchwork  34
    After Easter Sunday, 1956  37
    A Final Poem for You  39

**Sonata**
    Survivor  43
    Iron Lung  45
    Sonata  47
    directions for playing  51
    'Round Midnight  52
    The Craft  55
    At Seventy  56

**The Limits of Calculus**
    The Limits of Calculus  59
    Euphemism  61
    Picking Peaches  62
    Razor's Edge  64
    Leavening  66
    On the Anticipated Death of a Guinea Pig  68

**Climate Change**
    Climate Change  75
    Evergreen  76
    Wild Rhubarb  80
    She Folds Laundry  81
    Sound Byte 83
    The Apparent Immortality of Things  84
    Ghost  86
    Valentine's Day  87

**Theme and Variations**
    Theme and Variations for My Sister  91

## Apophenia*: An Apologia

> *All sorrows can be borne if you put them in a story or tell a story about them.* --Isak Dinesen

Some see Jesus in a grilled cheese.
When I first fell in love, I saw my beloved's name everywhere.
The world shimmered with dopamine, grew brighter.
Things light up when they connect.
You can see it happen in the brain, like orgasm.

An addict, I've sought the music of metaphor everywhere.
Synchronicity still sets me buzzing with delight,
its mysterious invitations exquisitely penned.
Part of how the world works,
they flare but cannot last.

I am Pisces with Taurus rising;
my lucky number is 27,
my spirit animal the hawk
(or the heron, depending);
once when I asked to be affirmed,
a feather appeared
at my feet.

I've thrown Hexagram 8 three times in a row.
Think of the odds.

The swirling linoleum on my bathroom floor
speaks volumes to me, especially
when stomach cramps strike.

After her son killed himself
my friend found a heartshaped rock,
took it as a comfort , direct from him.

But when her friends found heartshaped rocks too,
and sent them to her, her own no longer murmured.
Only then was she truly alone.

A bright, windless January day
seeks reassurance of connection.
Tonight's cold constellations might tell a tale.
We've peopled the cosmos with relatives,

named new dwarf planets *Makemake, Eris, Haumea, Ceres.*
Like us, they chatter: fly endlessly round something
they can neither escape nor understand.

My imaginary friend Marcia stayed in my orbit
sharing secrets 'til I passed
some nebulous transit of age and she drifted,
unnoticed, away into space.
Yet poets still root around for fresh links.
Happy as pigs in shit or clams in deep water,
they continue to make meaning
compulsory, compulsively secreting
concentric circles of something
pearl-like around pain, then
with ceremony
presenting them to us.

Buddhists call that compassion,
which requires imagination,
which calls forth from the bench
apophenia.

If I squint hard at the moon,
I can see whatever it is, my friend,
that tonight you see there.

Go ahead: tell me your story.

I will tell you mine.

*Inspired metaphors, paranormal beliefs, conspiracy theories, and delusional episodes may all exist on a single spectrum, recent research suggests. The name for the concept that links them is apophenia.

# The Beautiful Unnamed

## Quivira

*1541:*

Coronado rides in on horseback
looking for a legendary city of
gold, but finds only

a flow of grasshopper, turkey, deer,
migrating birds, sand, salt,
and savages in

moveable thatched huts, following bison.
Disappointed, he still names it *Quivira*
before returning to Spain.

*1875:*

Kiowa watch from lookouts while buffalo,
shot as vermin, topple to the earth
to rot where they fall,

skeletons so thick you can step one
to the other. Nothing turns, nothing
transforms. Stacked bones

mark the trackless prairie for schooners whose
dust Satanta, hidden in sandhills and tall
bluestem grass, marks.

Around one mound of bones--an
imaginary center--rises a town:
a sod hotel, one room to let,

blacksmith, a bank. Forts crop up against
Satanta, the Osage, Wichita, the Kansa,
scalplocks designating their bands:

Sky and Earth peoples, north and south,
they master seven stages of sacred knowledge,
dream dreams replete

with spirit of tree, sun, light, dark
painted on their shields, foretelling
a bleak future.

Because buffalo fed the Indian, hunters
wipe out the southern herd by '74,
Sheridan's winter campaign,

his Red River War. Other vermin
blocking the plow are destroyed for bounties:
dens of rattlers, prairie dogs,

the coyotes and jackrabbits my father still kills
forty years later. Onto the now
nearly empty prairie

steps the farmer who traces off claims
with a wagon wheel, broadcasts wheat
by hand, harvests

with cradle and scythe (sickle for the old
buffalo wallows and salt marshes),
grain threshed by cattle

or tossed in the air to blow away chaff.
Snake sticks line the walls of churches
bricked from red clay.

A few frame farm houses rise
from sacred cottonwood and willow. Women
share root-stalk

starts of roses hauled from Missouri, quilt,
preserve what they can, fear the Kiowa
who sometimes steal

them and their children, hate the prostitute
who steals their husbands. One night they march
her by the arm

to the depot, north end of town,
pay her exorbitant fare, push her
onto the train east,

along with a hundred cars of lucrative hides.
Most farmers endure until the drought
of '80, begetting poverty,

prairie fires, blizzards, tornados, typhoid,
snake bite, grasshoppers, nerves ratcheted up
by the south wind

that never stops: loneliness, silence, missed
music, missed shelter of trees. The turtles
find no water,

the silent trout curl up. The sheet water
of wells sinks from sight, wallows dry,
crack, fill with sand.

Feathered lances drip blood; Satanta
leaps to death from the penitentiary,
is buried deep without

paint, sacred bark or buffalo robes,
rocks, food, bow and arrow, pipe
or extra clothing.

Without proper ceremony, his skin
does not fall cleanly away
from his bones.

*1945:*

In the elevator south of town,
out by the other railroad tracks, across
the cracked tarmac

the old angled sidewalk bricks break,
sink into sand, the stored wheat settles,
the gold weight of it

falling to mold, falling to mildew save
for the constant thrum of a giant blower all
night all day

swirling the gathered grain, stirring, separating,
swirling, stirring, separating, within the closed
moist knuckles of

the elevator, whirling the clean grain
mounding in its concrete cup,
while a mile away

13

fungus visits three small graves
in less than a year; three small
cages of bone take longer

than flinted arrowheads to flake
away. Grain in the field sinks
to earth not to root

but to rot: spores, smuts, nothing
turns, nothing transforms: *fusarium, astilago
nuda, parasitic phytophthora.*

What is planted does not grow.
Wombs leak. Sperm does not engender.
Hope wanes.

I was conceived, it was whispered,
on the bank of the Rattlesnake
River, winding through

this reserve where my parents slept
on army cots under canvas
or, I hope, under

the bare sky where the lavish summer
constellations whirl: Lyra, given
by father Apollo to Orpheus,

poet and musician, rising late
on the horizon. As he might say,
I leapt into the cup

of my mother's womb, stopped its mouth,
began to weave my cage of bones.
For once, hope

did not die like a runt bounding
heedless from the dusty bed of a pickup.
Yet not being

born stolid and single-minded, I
was destined to disappoint.

*1975:*

My grandmother dies of cancer.
By her empty farmhouse
spring lilacs and lilies.

Busted farms are sold or taken over.
Farm Bureaus become conglomerates,
the latest

company store feeding on debt, offering
new weapons to eradicate new
vermin: pesticides,

anti-fungals, antibiotics, weed
killers. Atrazine contaminates
ground water.

Cancer appears in young families who pack
up and leave the cemetery where
a teddy bear swings like

a lynching over a grave. Growth hormones,
stimulants: rampant animals, deceptive
hollow lushness of wheat.

Refinery polluters turn hazardous
waste into silos of fertilizer to spread
over pastures.

The land is awash with illness. The tools
that wound and heal, gone: the disk of sun
no longer sacred,

the feathered lance in an undusted museum,
unvisited, the well a dry hole; no trickster
god to turn away pestilence.

Nothing turns, nothing transforms.
No one comes to ask whom we serve,
why we bleed.

*2013:*

My people are mostly gone. The town
has dwindled but nevertheless boasts a new
Christian coffeehouse

and a restored marble soda fountain.
And yet another remnant of the past
is to be "restored":

seas once rolled here leaving
salt as well as salt-tolerant grass.
And so this part

of the prairie, ignored, never leashed, spread out
and bloomed. For years deemed "wasteland,"
the salt marsh was left

alone to grow its network of roots
and seeds—its invisible bio-mass—
underground where

fire and drought were never dangers. Now
tourists, driving through this reserve
can look through binoculars

at the diorama without even
leaving their cars. But today, a Tuesday,
this twenty-two-

thousand-acre remnant of the past
is chained shut by a government standoff
led by the single-minded,

giving me leave to walk in alone.
Disappointing daughter, I do not
disappoint this land.

It simply accepts my brief return,
allows me to unfold my wings,
then lets me go.

Short, brown stems of sunflower stretch
all the way to that old cedar;
dry, silver shells of

milkweed have opened to the wind.
Endangered whooping cranes rest here
on their way to elsewhere.

This is a place for those who wander, whose
jeans will carry sand burrs to
another place: who,

like the wind, do not mean to stay.
I bless the cottonwood glinting gold,
the meadowlark riffling

his song, the gleaming bull snake
warming her long body in the sand
before slipping

into the tall grass. I mix
with all my relatives:
the many-minded--

mouse, deer, coyote, fox, rabbit,
plover, pelican and crane standing and waiting
for fish. I call upon

the four directions to exalt the huge
grasshoppers that terrified me as a child:
the crickets that calmed,

the locusts that buzz even above the wind;
the great blue herons like the one
tattooed on my shoulder;

I call upon the center and feel the sand
ever shifting under my feet; I look
up at the clean

sun and all my winged, boundless relatives
wheeling on the wind, redeemers all,
turning, readying the world

for change as I, too, turn, step
back over the chain across the road
and go.

## Chicken Dinner

Her husband of a year called her a *city girl*,
too squeamish to kill her own chickens.
So this morning, she shapes a sharp wire,
hook on one end, steels herself,
grabs three squawking hens, her best
layers, hangs them upside down from the
clothesline, works her way through the fluttering
flesh with the wire, cutting their stretched-out throats.

They still and bleed out while she gathers
herself, rinses her mouth, spits, re-pins
her hair. One by one she unclips
each pullet, slits it, tosses the glistening
entrails aside, saves livers, hearts,
gizzards. Then she turns to the plucking—masses
of dirty white feathers stick to her dress,
mouth, hair. Sweat trickles down
her forehead, into her eyes, burns.

                                                      Done,
she bathes the six-pound bodies in cool
well-water, pats them dry, is startled
anew to see their likeness to her baby
boy, still sleeping. When he wakes,
she'll put him to the breast, then lay him
down while she quarters those three
chilled torsos with a cleaver, rolls
breasts, necks, heart, thighs, liver,
legs, gizzard, wings in flour, fries
them hard in lard.

                        He tastes it, makes no comment,
bounces the baby a little too rough, a little too
hard, the child's head wobbling, spanking
new eyes opening wide.

                              She turns away
to the sink full of dishes, stares through the greasy window
at the fading farm, at the mongrel pup growling, pouncing,
flinging round the guts that very morning she'd thrown away.

**there is a wilderness**

there is a wilderness at edge of house
in small unmanaged shadows of neglect
where paint begins unseen to loosen or
a few weeds grow or unpruned boughs dip low
it can be glimpsed through unwashed windows where
things show not totally themselves and at
the backs of fallow cupboards or in shade
beneath those trees left to sprout at will
through holes in fallen fences or around
the rumpled rooms of those allowed to dally

only when flown there by the untamed wind
it trusts does wilderness take root in pots
or blow breathed time into the sweet
uncultivated cup of your hand

## A Child's Garden

Gardens grow themselves, sprawl
if unchecked: shadows merge,
boundaries dissolve and loose what's underground,
what's unremembered.

In the beginning, I remember iris,
tulips bent over me like tall colorful trees,
siblings who might do anything
behind our parents' backs
were they not root-restrained.

All I have learned since,
through working the earth,
can only be used on earth,
in light of day where things solidify,
stay separate.

The garden I've tended
all these years has hidden
thickets but even
the contents of thickets
have limits, Latin names, every
thing come down to itself,
language and knowledge shrink-
wrapping the fearful
metaphors of early knowing.

I've permitted few invasions, no
creepers to wrap round the frail-
shelled selves of the innocent.
It's where the fragile forgotten,
the unlabelled, the untagged
can come home free, be framed,
contained, come to light, or if they wish
can crouch in undergrowth till ready
to volunteer their names
known only to them unless
they choose to tell.

There is a place for cutting,
a place for cropping, a place
for composting what's past.

At the corner of my eye
on a hot June dusk, a few
new nooks reveal themselves
if not looked at direct,
like faint never-before-seen
stars in common constellations;
others we may never see;
what nameless, boundless thing
may yet emerge, both this and that,
unbidden, almost
indistinguishable from
the fecund, from
the feral dark?

**A Mother's Tale**

From their windows they always watched
her in her garden as she nurtured
the little plants:
breaking ground after last frost,
spading and hoeing the hard clumps
till only fine, sifted soil remained.

The seeds she sowed at new moon,
and watered with infusion of fish.
Into this coldness they came,
risking their wholeness to break ragged
root into furrows she had furnished.

She crooned to them, her children,
smoothed the way, coaxed them
up from night into the glory of day.
When the first tiny leaves
unlatched, moist, tender,
she saw the two — man and wife — watch,
drool over what was hers,
what she had toiled for: the fruit
of her perseverance and her love.

The night he came to snatch
the first pick she sat waiting,
old woman hunched under old tree,
trying to remember what it was to covet, to yearn.
Age sometimes teaches patience; gardening, endurance
through spells of apparent emptiness.

She was waiting when he climbed
the wall and took what was not his
to take. He did it for his wife, she knew,
but still he had to pay for her craving,
his indulgence.

*Your child for hers*, she challenged him,
rising as he prepared to leave.
Were he Pluto, she would not
let him steal her spring
for nothing.
Sealing the bargain as if she

were the devil, he fled,
leaving her garden torn,
ravaged, rootless, seedless,
long past the season for planting anew.
Holes gaped where her children were pulled
from their warm beds.

She sat down,
resting on scattered hopes,
began again
to wait.

ii.
She never thought to keep the child.
Her intent was just to borrow, bask
in her, then return
her to her sniveling mother.
But she was so happy
here with her that finally
she could not suffer her to go.

The little one loved the forest, the herbs
of her garden. She fed her pomegranates,
taught her what she knew
of growth and decay,
movement and rest.
She happily dug in the earth while the old woman
gathered stones for a tower.

She taught her all the songs she knew—
songs of hope, of sorrow—
strange, coming from soft young lips.
Yet she parroted perfectly
as rock upon rock piled into rings,
fit round them flawlessly
as a nest of iron.

At first they sheltered there
only in bad weather, brooding
together over rain, wind, stone.
But then they lingered longer and
longer, and one day, didn't leave.
The garden went to ruin,
overgrown, then a tangle
of briars and bare branches.
Inside was her spring:

she never tired of looking at her youth,
braiding her hair, combing through the thick

strands as she once had raked her garden.
She left their aerie only for tidbits
now and again to keep
the young one happy.

When she returned, played out, her daughter would lift
her with her braids as lightly as if
she were a trout hooked
in shallow water.

And so they lived.

iii.
*From craving comes grief,
from craving, fear;
she who is free from craving
knows neither grief nor fear.*

And yet she forgot, as one forgets the most
painful lessons.  In feeding her daughter's
every whim, she fed her own,
and thus they shrank to lazy sails slapping
in irons in the center of a windless sea.

But still her daughter sang.
And one day her chant lured another
into their doldrums.  Again
the old one's harvest was plundered.
An idle prince who had never posted seed
threatened to rob her of what she had raised,
pirate what she had reared.

Even after she cut the braids,
a sacrifice for them both,
they were not safe.

So they ran with the wind:
scratched, exposed
surviving on dark roots
and tiresome tears.

Tired, they came back
to that stairless tower

to await his inescapable
return. And when that fish struck bait,
climbed the now-dead hair, as they had done,
the old one threw him back, hard,
into the eye-scratching thorns.

Loss renders some compassionate.

His first glimpse of blindness
was her last remembered sadness.
Her daughter's lament now genuine, inevitably
they found each other — her tears piercing
the cloud of his sightlessness, his suffering
freeing her at last.

Seeing them there enfolded,
the old one longed for death,
like the barren vessel of earth in early winter
after its vines are cut down and thrown
into the fire.

And in that awful purity it came
to her how desolation,
how a perfect radical surrender sinks,
waits without waiting, sinks
inexorably to a tight tiny pellet, a ragged
packet, a kind of completeness
all its own.

## a stay

> *Who would have thought my shrivel'd heart*
> *could have recover'd greennesse?* --George Herbert, 1633

    The mound builder's ribs    curl round the ribs of a child
    under the earth, under    the new green; deep in a dry

        socket of bulb, a stalk    unfurls; how different
        from fall is spring,    though the same chill, softer,

    and the robins cluster in bare trees,    arriving, not leaving,
    generations removed    from the ones who sang

    the same, syncopated,    blessèd song to me as a child;
    I have come into    the light again; it is hard

    coming into the light    again; I blink stupidly,
    long to return to sleep    if just for a little while;

    but prospects    beckon in the very air
    I sniff like an old    spaniel, and it is hard

    to recall how    afraid I was, in
    the dark just past,    how I curled round my childish

fear, pulling the soft  earth round our shoulders;

        easy,    now;

it is still morning,    there will always be coffee,
in the morning, there    will always be a newspaper

    rustling up something    for the mind to knead, wrestle,
    stretch into new shape;    the cold nipples of redbuds

        tighten but will loosen    by afternoon; sunset's
        chaste aureola    will fade, back, into

        a fine April night;    the dark of spring is not to be feared;
        although everything    is hungry, even ravenous,

        for this little while    there is a stay

## The Beautiful Unnamed

> *Which is more inexpressible, the
> beautiful or the terrifying?* —Mary Ruefle
>
> *Death is the mother of beauty, mystical,
> Within whose burning bosom we devise
> Our earthly mothers waiting,
> sleeplessly.* —Wallace Stevens

i.
A mother of small children learns to forge
ahead to take the brunt of giant grasshoppers,

to capture inch-long centipedes
between Dixie cups to lob outside,

to pull, then pop ticks from baby scalps
before baby or bloody tick realized,

to chuck fragile daddy longlegs, apologetically,
from tents containing sleeping children,

to spray small limbs with DEET
against mosquitos that might carry virus,

to lure yellow jackets away from ice cream
to drown in sweetened drink.

A woman whose children are grown learns
to stop time: to watch a water strider

skate on liquid film; to feel a dragonfly's
neon needle stitch her close;

to stare while a lady bug gorges
herself on aphids, freeing buds in the garden

while a caterpillar spins itself
into a gold carapace that,

at least this time, turns clear,
swelling with wet, veined, fragile wings;

to note a bee humming above lovers
lying in soft purple vetch.

ii.

Nine hundred thousand species of insects
have been named; thirty million more

remain nameless (their fecundity reaching
far beyond Adam's span of attention).

Eve would gladly do it: take all
the time in the world to weave each new

name into the gauzy web of consciousness.
Naming calms, connects, comforts.  A child,

I remember rocking in pain, trying to
soothe my unnamed dis-ease,

hearing the threatening buzz of August locusts,
as my father crouched beside me,

impatient to convince that going to
the doctor would not be the death of me,

though it seemed to me to have been
the obvious cause of my sister's.

When he died, thirty years later,
in the hospital, at the very end,

the boy that he once was called
for his mother (by then many years

gone from cancer), to hold his hand, to sing
his name, perhaps to tell him once again

that he was loved and not to be afraid,
that it was safe to sleep.

iii.
Even grown children give us no
leave to die. And yet we do: shape-

shifting them into orphans who
must face, venture to touch, name

their dread, their beautiful Un-
Named, to sound its unsounded depth,

to stutter its new syllables in
unfathomable tongues: perhaps even,

uneasy humans on this still flowing,
happy earth, to hold out their arms

to claim what once so terrified.

30

*Family Snapshot*

**Family Snapshot**

You sit at the center:
the older sister,
the only one of us smiling,
the only one composed, gazing
direct into the eye of the camera
as if to affirm (though the rest of us
won't know this for another month):
your life stands complete.

The rest of us are caught
somewhere in the midst of our lives,
perched on the porch steps
(despite cracks in the cement).
We are blurred or blinking or glancing off
at the horizon or down at the dogs.
We have so many more things
to do. We can hardly wait to
shift, to be released from this enforced
immobility.

Grouped in still life, no one looks
at anyone else. No one touches. Unposed,
we suffer the shot in the thick of our
own separate, suspended lives.

Though we didn't see it then,
it's clear as the sky before a quake:
you were to become the core of our epic,
your approaching death
(forever after) our epicenter.

**Grounded**

Too young for the first war
too old for the second
my father flew only for fun.

Matching the Wright brothers'
audacity he hung around the hangar
outside the prairie town

'til the owner taught him
how to spin a wood propeller into life
how to lift off dirt runways,

loft into the south wind
at just the right slope without stalling,
how to sideslip sweetly back to earth.

Dipping long wings, he loved to bank,
buzzing his folks' farmhouse. He wanted
to ferry my mother up for a lark

but her knuckles would whiten like buttons
on the arms of the leather seat, her breath fading
to a tight wheeze. So she stayed fastened to the ground.

On he flew, weekends, freed from climbing poles
to fix phone wires. He'd soar up to smooth
unfettered air where nothing could stop him.

What stopped him
was my sister's death,
at sixteen, unimaginable.

He sold his plane to bury her, the costly coffin
covered up with dried buffalo grass and clods,
my mother's pearly knuckles tightening round his arm.

**Rose Sacrament**

The white wooden trellis bowed
under their red weight in late May.

My mother rose when it was not yet
blistering hot to cut the clusters,

bind them, fill a dozen coffee cans
saved all winter, covered with tinfoil.

My father drove, Mother and I always
sitting in silence through drought-ravaged

Kansas to the cemeteries of Great Bend,
Hutchinson, Stafford where

one or two  cans, topped off with warm
water from the lone tap in brown buffalo grass,

were screwed into the hard, cracked clay
next to each gray stone chiseled with a family name.

I found the roses' scent sickening,
overripe in the stifling, fenced

enclosures of loss. I would not shed
tears for my sister for many years.

I had never known grandparents.
As I fidgeted and played on stone lambs,

my mother stood silent before her best
offering, pricked fingers wrapped in Band-Aids.

As our car crunched away, I never looked back
but saw the roses already opening

their hidden parts, easy victims,
to the harsh wind. They would never

hold together long, readily offering up
their bared hips, their untethered ghosts.

True sacraments are hard to come by.

I should have paid closer attention.

**Patchwork**

Scraps like quilt patches
piece into patterns--

Wedding Ring, Crazy,
Grandma's Fan, Memory Charm--

bits unused, outgrown, unfinished,
basted together with tiny stitches,

themselves part of the plan,
part of the motif, seen anew

like the delphinium called
"larkspur" by my mother,

delicate, hard to grow from seed,
its blossom-laden spikes so heavy

they bend or break before blooming
unless staked stiffly with twine,

even in death magnificent, its many
waves of deepsea blue folding in, reflecting

a grey change of weather and then
at collapse, the trio of dolphins

for which it is named, suddenly revealed, leaping
from the spent nectary of its very center,

but only at the very end of its life,
each patch is seen as for the first time,

set into a new design, like the blossoms of
elms she said she'd never noticed 'til she accepted

that blossoms could be green, could see
the bristle stuck in the oiled skin of the painting

the accidental tick of bow against the cello's mahogany back
the hard thump of ballerinas' feet that

call back the illusion  created by frame and stage,
could see that transcendence is made of nothing

but the hair and wood and bone that limit it and yet
a poem must pass, like a quilt--

Bear's Paw, Ocean Waves,
Red Brick Road, Pinwheel--

through the coarse fine needle of the poet
like seed through shit, though she

hated that word, through
the lumpy messy chalice of earth,

no scrap thrown away, each
waiting in the sack to be selected,

reseeded, revised for possibility, how small
glances, she said, can fill the file of a whole life,

the way snow lies along a branch,
the sturdy curve of a neck

as someone stares out a window,
the sound of a bird whose name

she never knew, the belief
that she will never understand,

puzzles someone has to show her
how to solve, how time

curves space, what happens
if you move forward faster

than you fall, filling the quilt with variations
upon variations she finds lying

under her fingers; how the frame swells
with the texture of her thoughts, how

the universe expands, creating out
of nothing new space between galaxies

ex nihilo  ex nihilo  ex nihilo  her
fool calls, smiling just

out of sight, how years go by and
her hands still weave in the same

lucky mistakes, manifest the same
peculiar elegance of imperfection, which,

when hemmed by community, quilted,
softened by some magic of connection,

tag ends of gossip and new
combinations of stories, forms

the passagework for draping  wedding beds,
childbeds, everyday beds—

Plain and Simple, Spinning Spools,
Sunny Days, Love's Delight.

**After Easter Sunday, 1956**

Idling in our new Buick waiting to leave
the parking lot with all the other colossal

cars exhaling soft invisible exhaust
into the thickening shadows of spring, the birth

season of small creatures not yet blighted
except by their own natures, my father lights up,

my mother stares as always inward to
her draped casket of sadness, me thinking,

from the back seat, my eleven-year-old
ankles encased in hose and properly crossed,

how the day I die will be a day
just like today, how each day

will become inexorably today, will
slide into yet another day

like beads on (we had no
rosaries) the cheap steel chain

clasping my cold war ID tag
tucked under the thin dress, or

better yet, I muse, like walking
backwards inbetween drops of rain,

or though there are no computers
then, like plunging link through endless

link until the day I die.

And it will be, I remember thinking
with some horror, on a day

just as real as today, when
I sit, without a seat belt, alone

on the wide back bench, quiet
so as not to startle those two

silent anxious adults scanning their own
bound worlds, so as not to call

their attention, though caged, so as
to be left alone, young spring

creature camouflaged inside its own
life, blessed with the instinct

to be very still, waiting to hang
the sweaty dotted swiss up to dry,

waiting to slip on shorts, waiting
as patiently  as I can until it's safe

for my real life to begin.

**A Final Poem for You**

Fog beads the iron fence's crop
    of spider webs.

I trip over your stone trying to find it
    in thickening fog,

biting air for a moment warmed, immobilized,
    on the late winter prairie.

I stand red poppies, red carnations
    in the gritty brass urn

I turn right side up. They aren't as sweet
    as the wind-whipped

red roses our mother scythed for you,
    dead at sixteen.

After all, perhaps she was not too
    protective, our mother;

maybe from the time they placed you carefully
    in her arms she sensed

the tenuousness of your touch. Maybe she took
    one look at you

and knew you were fair game for all
    earth's predators and

hovered, as if her worry could protect
    you, baring its blunt

ineffectual fangs at the twice-
    paralyzing virus.

Finding your sheer prom gloves inside
    her drawer, I could not

slip in three fingers, your hands so small,
    the one leg stunted

at ten, the other deliberately broken to match.
    Fifty years after

that final, lung-stilling, brutish,
    uncontrollable summer of

polio, I can breathe deep, speak
    your name, say goodbye.

Our mother and you have unveiled to me the griefs
    of Persephone and Demeter, their mutual

loss, but never the second half of the myth:
    their reunion, unless

it was in her death or the births
    of my three daughters:

an embarrassment of riches. I marvel
    at their sturdy legs,

large hands, difficult tempers, but not
    out loud. Who knows

what weakens the spirit's resolve to stay?
    what broadcasts

'desirable' to Hades' nearby realm?
    I stoop beside the furrow

through which you sank to obediently eat death's seed.
    My blooded flowers stand

stiff-stemmed with heavy, fleeting visibility,
    ineffectual sentinels.

From miasma neither do poems much protect,
    seen and seeing for only

a little way before they too fly
    apart in the teeth of the wind.

## *Sonata*

## Survivor: Banking on It

*After many lives, maybe something changes.* —Louise Glück

i.
She was my babysitter, bodyguard,
my buffer between me and our parents. In return
I brought her napkins of crumbled cake from birthday
parties, crayoned for her the letters of my name.

Had I not been held down
in 1952 and pumped full
of gammaglobulin I should have died,
would have caught the polio that killed my sister.

Before, I didn't really know
that anyone could die; after, my body
quickly learned: stomach cramped and skin
peeled; to swallow and to sleep were perilous.

Hunched over my journal, I kept secret
the metaphors that came to me as cure.
Re-caulking with words what had been nearly swamped,
poetry's rites ferried me from death.

Pedaling furiously toward the piano teacher's
house, practicing daily until they pried
me away, playing for time, my greed
for music's waves carried me toward life.

ii.
Here's a hard one: what happens, in the
end, to the art a survivor
creates? Is it carefully gathered in and
counted to pay life's debt to the dead

for years cut short? the dead who spend,
alone, what passes for time? Has it
been enough to justify *my*
survival so far? How much farther?

Or is it just as carefully hoarded, talents
allotted to my next life, not
to have to begin again at zero, notes and
lines gifted to new fingers, new

voice, bearing compound interest?
I envy those free to improvise,
for the fun of it, a riff, a life, simple interest
coined and plunked freely into the collective.

But for me, creating is serious business.
Her sweet, empty mouth still hungers for my
crumbs. If I save anything for myself,
it's to an unnumbered, sequestered account.

No one must ever know if, when, or
what I cash in.

No one must ever glimpse the furtive, unearned
joy I take.

**Iron Lung**

Events leave only faint,
pale imprints on my hippocampus,

the heavy-footed goddess of memory
forever tip-toeing, slipping

her tap shoes off at my door.
The rare visuals I hoard,

misshapen, bubbled beads picked up
with primitive pinchers, are strung

into worried, storied, static
frames of film: frozen moments

when my sister was about
to leave me behind: running

down a stair to a party;
turning away, masked, with friends

to trick-or-treat; in her coffin,
dead of polio, dressed in lilac

tulle as if for her prom:
me insisting to my parents,

*look, she's breathing*; then,
scolded, *but what will we do with her things?*

My body evokes a touch more:
twist in the gut, jagged warning

of aura before migraine,
but also, my child's hand

as she moved its chubby parts
expertly into a finger game;

my mouth around half a sticky
red popsicle as our

legs brushed, making warm
patterns in the dust with our toes;

the bellows of my ever-vigilant
lungs breathing exhaled life

into her now,
into her then,
into her now.

**Sonata**

i. exposition

This is about a girl at the piano.

This is about flight.
This is about practice.
This is about the practice that makes possible
the flight.

This is about beginning, the first
part of the pattern when it seems
you can do anything,
take any form:

first stroke on canvas,
first kiss,
first caress of a chord.

This is about the possibilities
of small hands.

>    Daughter of my body, you sit rigid
>    before the keyboard, balking at what
>    it requires of you.
>
>    Haltingly, you try a melody,
>    slump, correct a wrong note, sigh.

A cripple came to me in my dream,
trying to keep up, demanding my love.
I wanted only to be free.

The music perches on the rack
like air before a flight,
the keys grounded before me like
planes in a port.

>    You begin.

ii. development

>    Daughter of my spirit,
>    I feel your hands grow excited,
>    sensitive, quiver
>    with unsung music.

So it was for me when our house,
saddened by my sister's death,
permitted no dance.

I lugged my yellow books
to the teacher's house after school
where she recognized
at once what no one else had seen:
my love of flight and
my lack of control. She hooked
me by the back of my vision,
made me account for carelessness.

Made me slow down.
Made me lumber through exercises
invented by men so old
I never knew
their faces.

>    I sat rigid
>    before the keyboard,
>    balking at what
>    it required of me.

Over and over, trying
to get it right, at last
there came moments when even
the most difficult arpeggios
spun out like silk from my fingertips,
when playing was like wings
effortlessly brushing bells:

two hands in consort, soaring
through a forest of intricate harmonies,
not caring for the names
of notes, not needing me, really,
at all, except to get out of their way.

iii. recapitulation

Then there are times when
fingers are stiff wooden
clubs translating nothing,
a dream in which
I can't remember the way home,
the swift flight of fingers
crashing to earth,
creatures that never
knew how to dance.

> Daughter of my heart, you sit
> rigid before the keyboard, balking
> at what it requires of you.

I, too, have stamped my foot at God,
demanding respite, seeing no progress,
pleading for release.

So was pregnancy:
a huge helplessness
before the creation
of someone else.

Limitation and failure and waiting:
time and space and size were
barriers to the ultra-
sound of boundless music.

> When you were small
> I did not play at all.

> Dust sifted between keys,
> which you tentatively touched
> with sticky jam.

Secretly gardening, I
cultivated beauty, hoarded
landscapes improvised
rock by rock,
seed by seed,
note by unheard note.

Now I understand
> when you want to shut the door,
> grow incensed when I sing along.

iv. coda

Melodies remain; words fade.

    Daughter of my soul,
    at last understanding imperfection,
    we honor the best we can do
    done over and over until
    we surpass ourselves, leaving earth,
    unaware.

    Now am I lost in play while you
    cup hands and shout at me while
    pots boil over.

A woman, playing
alone, composes
herself, knowing
there is always more
to draw upon.

Early or late
makes no difference.

Space, and time, and
limitation, and failure,
are means.

To see that truth
is to see
the gate in the wall,
sequel, reassurance
there is yet more,
like flight,
to pull from impossibility,
from inaudible frequencies,
into the reach
of real.

## directions for playing

life should be lived legato* and
rock climbing sure as hell better
be legato for there is danger
leaving the ground on your own and
swimming is legato only because of
water which is very legato but not so much
as smooth crystal-linked ice or as staccato**
as rain beginning to pelt your head
                              learning anything
including how to be married is staccato at first though
the goal is legato but that takes practice which hopefully
will stitch together the staccatos and draw
them tight to the point where the strokes
are not even seen beneath the surface or
in the seam
              there are those who stumble
up the stairs to enlightenment young and never
look down and those who take to water as babes and can't
remember when they knew anything but
legato
    the woman in the lane next to me with her smooth enjambment
between laps surely is one who started swimming when wet
behind the ears long after polio left its jagged blip on
the surface of some historical pool but for me learning
has been a life of sitting anxious on the edge and wanting it
enough to be willing to die if needs be while slapping
together staccatos hit or miss mostly not
getting it right rising and indeed plunging but not
in a good way though my crawl finally cobbled
together a compromise of air and water that
has got me eventually to the end
                              and in the end
perhaps it's not anything we do ourselves to connect
just life sooner or later tired of expressing as separate
particles rising then falling back effortlessly into waves
like that magician's trick of stuffing scarf after scarf into a
fist then smiling and teasing out a billow of graceful knotted silk
or faceless paper-dolls with just the tiniest point of join

*in a smooth, even style without any noticeable break between the notes
**composed of abrupt, disconnected parts or sounds

## 'Round Midnight

> ...let us take the garments of the dark about us
> slowly and deliberately, without haste and without fear.--
> Alexander McCall Smith

REM cycle i:

Step out of the body
for a little minute, having
worked all day to earn

this right; step out
of the score for an instant;
stand up and play your

fluid truth. Improvise:
fill the silence, the space left
for you and your solo,

constructed and construed in that fine
pandemonium of the moment.
Become the spindle for those nets of notes

swaying round you, for those
whose sleeping bodies dance to your pulse.
Thelonius Sphere Monk and Johann

Sebastian Bach lean out of their shadows
watching, listening, tapping their slippered feet,
you the one stepping up, now,

you the one in the spot light,
the whorl of your finger prints
on the keys, the snip of your

DNA in the mix,
dissonance and silences
honored within the math and

intricate physics of music,
keeping the devil on edge,
keeping sadness at bay.

Waking cycle i:

Today you read that cancer is
a riff on the body's cells: the daughter cells,
the daughters of the daughter cells
into which a malignance sings its
repeated aria, independent
of the group, the agreed-upon
structure, and will not
sit down but keeps on
playing, perseverating , far
after everyone else has
stopped listening, gone home.

REM cycle ii.

*A flowing flock of dark starlings poises
to tip, stretches like a rubber band,
then suddenly shifts, noiseless,
darting together, diving, fanning out*

*onto the stage of this unfastening minute
where also creeps the ad-libbing world,
demolishing the limit
of what we thought was possible, uncurling.*

*At night, colored surfaces are dull.
How do birds and squirrels survive such cold?
You keep the feeders full.
The owls that kill and rats that scrounge are bold.*

*Surprise encircles our little selves.
The rhyme comes out of nowhere, as it were,
as if the poem were made by elves
though, in a quantum field, there is only blur.*

Waking cycle ii:

You pull remnants of the dream
'round you, watch the sun come,
without haste or fear, to this
cold day to light up
the morning urgencies of every
wild creature: to eat and drink,
to frolic and be free of malady.
The dreaming tortoise of time

covers us all with its crazed shell,
protects the genesis of melody,
dance, poetry, and
the murmurations of starlings,
keeping sadness at bay.

You roll out of bed, barefoot
in your cold kitchen, drink your coffee
and watch bird by awkward bird
land on the line of your ledge,
fiercely strut, squawk,
await impatiently its rightful place
at the day's funnel of seed.

The piano calls you, again,
to solitary practice and today's
precious measures of mistakes.

## The Craft

> *The lyf so short, the craft so long to lerne*—Chaucer

Meaning arrives slowly,
a song from great distance,
a breeze passing over
ditch water. While it lasts,
you lean into its shiver.

You do not master a craft;
it brushes you with surprise.
And if you tender the tips of
your most hopeless longing,
your most stubborn faults,

craft will bind them into a beauty
so dense, so pure, so rare, so common,
you will find yourself cast into a spell of
amazement, of gratitude so deep
you will feel forever young in its thrall.

You do not master a craft;
you are the village fool that fumbles,
falls, breaks the cask: then frees,
attends, willingly surrenders to the genie
everything you have and are:

your seed, your root, your core,
your insatiable need.

**At Seventy**

At seventy, the thing she wanted
to learn was to dive:

to tuck her chin to her chest, between
her outstretched arms and to fall

headfirst toward the bottom she had both
feared and yearned for since she had

first seen water—the still pool
untouched, unrippled, heavy with meaning

and promise: to feel its cool caress, hear
the bubbles of breath leave her body, see

the illusion of being enclosed utterly by blue;
to know that she could aim her body down,

then up, and it would joyously comply,
her remaining breath buoying her up, up,

up to break the surface of the old familiar
world as if rising from sleep; it was something

like flying, she thought, something like
taking off from one medium and trying on

another, shedding one set of rules for a second:
one which both frightened and enthralled,

a kind of life to which she had always been born,
on the edge of which she has been forever poised.

# The Limits of Calculus

## The Limits of Calculus

Calculus, according to my father,
born a hundred years ago, could perfectly
plot the velocity of change for everything
that began to move at more and more
amazing speeds in the next fifty years.

Yet even apparently standing still,
he and I had trouble taking each other's
measure except in terms of our own positions
and, as relativity predicts,
those measurements never matched up.

He spoke best the jargon of mathematics,
and in his workshop handled transistors, transformers,
resisters whose quirks and imperfections he
could easily calculate.
                              For me, he
remained out there somewhere,
a cloud of electrons round which I constantly buzzed,
trying to get a fix. I could plot
the simple outer changes in his formal
portraits snapped at points over the years:
the high-school boy with the combed-back
bend of pompadour, the concave
chest of the chain-smoking years, the knotted
tie below the down-turned curve
of his tightening, ever-thinning mouth.

I must have seemed a once-in-a-lifetime
comet come whizzing by, out of sight
much of his life, a swarm of bees or charged
particles for him to dial through like static,
frustrated but in the end unscathed.

At the end we missed connection, a final
reckoning to ease the unavoidable
and ironic fission. For him, my sentences
just didn't parse; for me, Newton's
formula failed to gauge the thrust, the
accelerating, separating parabolas
of our lives.

We might have met comfortably
in a quantum, relative world or even
in this poem where irreconcilable,
immeasurable differences are only to be
expected, some say even integral
to the chain: to that unbreakable,
some say odd and inexplicable,
hidden kinship of things.

## Euphemism

              Sitting on the edge of the
bed at the nursing home
my father said how,
panicked, he'd groped his mind for
the word for the thing you stick in
your mouth to see how hot you are.
He told me he knew if he just
sat still, like a spaniel it
would come to him.
                    It used to be,
the tail ends of our statements rose
to meet us like retrievers or
the anchored ends of bridges.
                              Yesterday,
my husband said he couldn't say
what "euphemism"meant, which startled
him, a piece of the known world
falling away. He knew it specified
saying something other than what
one meant but he dis-remembered
why.
          Death was once
construed as an image in
our daughter's dream: the moment you lean
forward to kiss a waiting lover,
the moment you know you are falling
in love.
              As I watched
the white coats inside-out
her dirty satchel in the bare
room we had driven her to, taking
away the thing that you shave with, the little
things that you rub against rough to make fire,
the limbs of language dismembered,
bled, fled like wild
things dissolving before me,
like monsters in movies that aren't
real, where what you've always
walked on falls away and families
run on air or have to leap
to reach, to grasp the last word that's left,
that's leaning, precious, precarious, toward them.

**Picking Peaches**

My mother remembered one beautiful day.
She pilgrimed with others to pick bushels
of peaches in the public orchard, and after,
she would can jam and bake pies,

but that wasn't the point. The point was
the glory of that day, the rare harmony
with her husband and their friends, the warmth and
lusciousness of the just-picked fruit.

For once, she allowed herself happiness,
or rather, delight overtook her.
But next year when they returned, angels
of Eden barred the way with swords: the day

wasn't quite as warm, her husband in a
foul mood, the peaches sour, pithy,
overripe. She always talked about
her disappointment as if she just couldn't

understand why, once allowed,
a particular pleasure couldn't be recaptured,
but bounded away into the past.
Yet she rounded up sorrows easily,

pecks of sad skinny cats always
at the back door, a yowling litany
she thought would leave her alone, if she fed them.
Instead, they grew sleek and fat. I saw

they would never leave a good thing
once they found it. My mother-in-law never
used any beautiful thing she was given
but closed them all carefully away in drawers.

Released into dementia, she was never
disappointed by lining up present and past.
"What a beautiful garden," she would exclaim from
our porch, while she could still speak. And

a moment later, "What a beautiful garden,"
not knowing she was repeating herself.

The Buddhists say to meditate on death,
so to self-medicate against

forgetfulness of impermanence, a kind
of caffeine or nitroglycerin for the
soul. But like most mothers I have
no need to meditate on impermanence—

have seen moments snatched, fade, sucked
away right before my eyes, have
no belief that today's delights will last
past this turn of the kaleidoscope.

It seems joy is just something we pick.
I used to lick the warm fuzz of dust
off my mother's closed bedroom door.

My mouth still waters at the thought.

**Razor's Edge**

You are almost grown
and in another country but
in my dream, in stealth,
I am cleaning your room.

I am a guest, and your friends
and roommates are everywhere.
Music is playing and plans
are being laid. You love me

but don't really know what
to do with me now that I've come.
You are a blur of motion
as I sit in a corner watching

all this life surge round
until I cannot stand it and start
to clean the fierce bedlam of your room.
Just to straighten, I tell myself,

just to sort things into piles. But
then I am stripping your bed, unearthing
the stash of stuffed animals under the dingy
sheet and forcing them into make-shift stalls.

With deep, undeniable pleasure, I
collect all your dirty shirts and socks,
and when all is matched and arranged, I look
for a broom, a mop. But the ground-in grime

of many youths, the indifference of many years,
is too great. Even if a cleaning
apparatus unexpectedly
appeared, it could only scratch the surface.

So my still-sleeping eyes strain
to straighten the casual chaos of your dresser—
a tiny carved white owl (its feathers
donned for bravery), the plumed jewelry,

scarves, the ashes from spent incense,
and what I know is always there--
that stalker leaning against a lamppost--
that silver, single-edged razor blade.

Even in my dream I know that what
I'm doing is wrong but can't stop. If only
I knew how to intercede, what
totem needs to be appeased, what

sacrifice to burn before it, what
new name to call forth:
if only some warning, some cold call
of snowy owl, weren't prodding me

to wake, wake up,
wake up now.

**Leavening**

Listen: everything can be used.
Everything is a path;
even your grief

can curl into the center
where like a shard
of beached glass

worn that way and this
is wave softened at last.
Begin anywhere

and watch it start
to roll, to wash
into something

else, somewhere away
from the static ground
of winter doubt into the chaotic

order of a cloudy spring. Only part
of the picture, peace
spreads slowly.

The debris of self-pity,
consumed by the winter-
famished, is the leaven

by which we rise, the tiptoe lightning
of laughter on the edges of fronts,
the thresholds of thunder on which, teetering, we see.

Look: here is balm for your tangled
clump of self-sorrow, this flight of steps

stretching from the bare bottom
of this ridiculous snuffling pig

of our humanity to what is called
paradise. Hung on this laddered cross

between fleet summer grass
and ancient flare of stars

we look down, up:
where build our home?

Come: rising
from cavern to heaven,

mounded earthen birds

between soil and sky,
we escape:

unpinioned, we grow wings.

Yeast bubbles in our bones
which lighten, fill

with air. Our throats

inflate with song. We flow
into feathered capes,

sacrifice sorrow; birds of flame,

we are restored in ash-filled nests;
we soar, doves of mourning.

Carving air with wings we learn

to slip qualms, recover stalls,
move from here to there

by naked intention.

Called down to bury her once more,
we forfeit flight but never lose

the leavened feel of space,

the sill of sight, the truth
of unthinkable migrations

height substantiates.

**On the Anticipated Death of a Guinea Pig**

i.
My daughter named her Mimi.

A rare albino, nearly blind,
she never gentled to human touch,
disappointing my girl who wanted
something to cuddle when
depression loomed.

I offered to care for her when my daughter
left behind this all-but-empty
nest.
                    At seven, Mimi
has known nothing but a cage.
Now she has spawned a tumor
and is losing her hair.

ii.
Curious, I read that
*these domesticated descendants of Andean*
*rodents have never existed naturally*
*in the wild. Domesticated for*
*biological experimentation,*
*they have been largely replaced*
*by other rodents--mice and rats.*
*The longest living guinea pig*
*survived for nearly 15 years.*

iii.
Mimi chirps with measured joy
at her morning timothy hay
with chrysanthemums and
her gourmet Kaytee mix of
sun-cured alfalfa, ground
oats, hulled sunflower,
split peas, dehydrated carrots,
shelled peanuts, dried
bananas, raisins, pumpkin seed,
dried papaya.
                    She struggles
in my hands as I lift
her out, once a week,

and place her on a clean towel.
Donning a latex glove, I scrape,
then pour the urine and feces-
soaked bedding into a bag,
swab the bottom of her cage
with baking soda and an anti-
bacterial wipe; refill it with
sweet-smelling shavings of pine.
She scurries back into her dirty blue
plastic house as soon as she can.

iv.
*In some cultures they are rubbed
against the bodies of the sick
for healing. The animal may
also be cut open
and its entrails examined
to determine whether the cure
was effective. These methods
are widely accepted in
many parts of the Andes,
where Western medicine is distrusted*,
soothing ourselves as we do
with the likes of lexapro,
xanax, paxil, celexa, prozac,
zoloft, cymbalta, effexor, elavil,
nardil, tegretol, lithium, valium,
klonipin, wellbutrin and abilify.

It is said that *single guineas
are prone to anxiety…. and in Switzerland,
it is illegal to keep just one.*
But I have no evidence
of Mimi's distaste for being alone.
Her litter mates are long gone.
She self-grooms her few remaining
patches of white hair.

Mornings I switch on the radio
for her: patterns of silence and sound
to mimic my daughter's presence.

v.
Today, taking a break from
clearing out our home of 25
years, I read that human
pacemakers can be

cruel cages, denying those
who have 'fallen into' dementia
the freedom of a 'natural' death.
I am glad that neither Mimi
nor I has a pacemaker.

Lunching on a cold chicken
leg, I read that I might
live longer on a diet
high in protein.

*Guinea pig meat is high
in protein, low in fat and cholesterol
and tastes like the dark meat
of chicken. Traditionally, the guinea pig,
or* cuy, *was reserved
for ceremonial meals
by indigenous people in the Andes.
One famous painting of
the Last Supper in the main
cathedral in Quito shows
Christ and the twelve disciples
dining on* cuy.

       I finish my lunch.

I toss old letters
into Ziplocs; cram undated
photos of our amazingly unique
children-that-were into
Walmart bins; long-ago
wedding clothes into under-the-bed
coffins; jettison years of dusty
notebooks, dream journals,
textbooks, lecture notes,
out-of-date clothes, forgotten bedding
with mouse droppings in their folds.

And so we live out our lives.

My house is scrubbed clean.

My litter lies in knotted bags on the curb.

I long to take a trip.

vi.
*A guinea pig is the first
creature to travel to the Wood
between the Worlds in
The Chronicles of Narnia.*

*Guinea pigs have been launched
into orbital space-flight
several times, with successful
ocean recoveries.
                They are
exceedingly good swimmers.*

                            But Mimi
is going nowhere until,
as the vet prophesied,
she will stop drinking water.

Then I will lower her gently
into a carrier and take her
on a short journey, probably
to end in our nearly-filled
backyard plot already sheltering
a gerbil and two beloved dogs.

viii.
Today is Sunday: the day to clean
her cage. I click on a channel
of light rock. We experiment
with the Four Seasons'
"Big Girls Don't Cry"
while I once again change
her stinky soiled bedding .

As I take that bag
along with another of my
own outworn paraphernalia
to the bin, I tell myself
that this time she struggled
less as I held her
briefly to my chest.
Her hair is growing back.

We eat. We sleep. We anticipate.

Ineluctably we come to care.

## Climate Change

**Climate Change**

So slowly some clouds slip across the sky
you'd never know they were moving, save

for the frame of window, from wings of which
swallows dart, disappear, and maple

seeds, not quite alive, spin
presumably to earth where in hot Junes

of 1950 Kansas they crunch beneath
my bare feet. What is a life

without a frame to set against its motion?
Or a moving frame to capture our stillness?

Not much has changed since 1952.
Everything has changed--dying become small,

personal: quakes, comets, wildfires, floods, droughts
come, not to mark any particular passing,

not even elephants' or polar bears'. We are
so many humans now, the world a wiki

correcting itself, growing around impediments
like tree root while, blind traffic officers,

we try to direct with our white gloves.
Through the window frame, layers of cloud

appear photo-shopped: some permanent as
wallpaper; others transparent fleeting, flashing forward.

Any cry from what burns, drowns, or
disappears beyond the frame is blocked

by double-glazed glass, yet reaches the parts that mourn,
unable to see whence or whither.

**Evergreen**

i.
From branch to stem to needle we grow,
shoots predictable and unpredictable as stars.

Her winter garden hisses with snow
rattling bleached bones of cone-

flower and verbena, cowled
roses dark in their March hollows,

goldenrod roots tangled,
massed under the frozen crust.

Second full moon in March,
blue moon suddenly blooms

like the first moonflower
on a trellis, climbing

an invisible vine.  Such moons
she has always watched swell

and wane, hoping that in their dark
doubled ridges, the things she planted

would thrive.  But Athena still springs
full-blown from her father's bright

brow, no mother to let her
lag, wax slowly, muse,

be a little girl whose dreams
grow new rooms looming

suddenly past the wall where
before there was no door,

but now are rooms within rooms,
fractal rooms of infinite length.

We have not dreamed large enough.

ii.
Twilight dallies with the toes of girls
loafing on curbs, brown arches caressing
dust.

Small green doublets of sunflowers,
sprung volunteer, turn likewise,
young,

blind, to setting sun. Full
moon rises unseen
over the stems

of their backs, in the east, dawning.
Inside, she washes dishes
at her kitchen sink.

Her heart rises, glimpsing moon's porcelain
globe before it cracks among trees.
She turns

back to rinse the precision of
each white cup, hangs the blue
linen cloth

carefully to dry, slips out
to calmed dusk to idle with her daughters
dreaming a garden.

iii.
She muses: we thought
the world would change,
we young and noisy feminists,

but we have slackened,
the waves subdued now,
an occasional stridency

swallowed, like a gull's
cry by the dark.
But today somewhere

a woman's clitoris was sliced
from her body, some-
where tonight a woman

walking stares at
a radium-infested field,
somewhere today

a caged dog was killed
by white coats,
somewhere tonight

are women and their daughters
draped and locked away
from sight of men and moon.

iv.
Receding snow releases scent of broken
spruce boughs brooding over red

fists and then the softening mudras of peony
stems as well as small carcasses gathered

lovingly to earth.  The living dog
lying in spring sun licks the crevices

and furrows of her palm and so weaves
kith into the woof of poem just as

earth weaves death into the warp
of spring.  The girls go on playing

with dust and the woman with water and
from their play rises creation that matters

the world, which withers without the muddy
juice of their play though it lead to nothing

but deep-winding pleasure.  Earth opens
to the dark newness of moon and to green

seeds ever so small they vanish,
shoots of stars, into the vast imaginary

lines of her palm.  She folds leeway
back into her veins, does not term

her creations, but dreams lavish
iterated wonder into moon's

blue light, which, rising
ever again and new, wicks the world.

## Wild Rhubarb

Once upon a time
in the wilderness of puberty

a girl swore to strive
for perfection in all things.

She vowed to excise
the outlaw in herself, so

began to weed.
One day she knelt,

pulled off the toughest plant's
toxic leaves, then spied

the wrist-thick rhizome
burrowed in red, hard clay.

She began to dig,
and as she dug was learning something

about determination,
about the deep, wild beauty

of imperfection: that
one day girls like her,

who seem to submit, whose minds
are never allowed to gather light,

will run renegade,
and through the densest matter, despite

desecration by
the fiercest gods, thrust forth

from earth's succulent belly
lush throngs of thicker, greener,

even darker, shoots.

**She Folds Laundry**

Sun-dried shriveled hands
flashing rings with sprung settings,
they have come to this:
humped over an old-woman smell,
folding other people's laundry.

Unhurriedly she smooths,
presses each piece,
flattens, turns,
multiplies dimension.

Long fingers prop fabric
into fanciful forms:
a long-beaked bird,
the dragon in the mirror,
the dog flopping asleep on her bed,
the hornet bumping against glass.

She looks back down
at the clean towel on her lap
considering its shape
while a spider in the corner
crochets its template of web.

In silent mimicry she thinks,
like you they crimp possibility
into the same old nets,
tuck thought into tight
packets of words: hook, weave,
pleat from their programmed spinnerets.

She smiles, creasing
the soft mesh of diapers
warm, soft and sweet,
seducing the cheek.

Flesh flowers and withers,
fills and wrinkles,
time doubling back materially
as sideways she sees

her own young mother through the door
watch her
with that worried look.

The weave of her love would never stretch
as far as this old woman, she thinks:
these folds no longer dimpled, kissable,
but slack, hung from brittle bones.

She stacks intricately plaited textiles
back into the basket so that light
tips radiance cross many layers.

It will not last,
she thinks.
The moment it is donned
it comes undone,
the inexact geometry
of tomorrow's universe
unfolding.

I ply cloth, but
who has shrunk this
life called mine
into such pinched shape
even light can't love?

**Sound Byte**

The news factoid on the drive-
thru bank's tiny screen reads:

"Sound is the last sense to go
when one dies." While my car exhales,
I think of the fact that the

Sumerian words for ear and wisdom are
the same. I think of Dickinson's *uncertain*

*stumbling Buzz* ; but it could be a crow's
raw rasp, lookout in the pine,
warning of something huge bearing down.

It could be my husband's voice, my child's,
the opening bars of Puccini's *Sola,*

*perduta, abbandonata,* or the happier,
even syllables of rain. Or
the sharp bark of my aging dog

startled from sleep; an approaching siren;
or, hurrying, bullying, hustling me through,

the fierce blast of an impatient horn.

**The Apparent Immortality of Things**

Sometimes I catch them at it
alone in the house

catch sound of their stillness
their capacity to wait

their pointing to something beyond
passage, something

beyond loss. There is
beauty in their

silence, the way they allow the
slipcover of light

to flicker, to play over
their surfaces but never

themselves alter, never
change. Of course,

they do. But I rarely
see it: the slow

settling of grime into
a surface, the bleaching and

thinning of fabric by sun.
But to me

they just remain, never
moving, whether I'm

there or not, the same
when I return

from a day or a week or a month
away in the sweaty,

swirling world of eating
and breathing and pain.

Here they still are,
neither precisely

dead nor living,
stretching out,

present participles,
constant as mothers,

light and air and time
mapping such

tiny inroads my eyes
are too big, too

young, too tender
to see.

**Ghost**

On the far side of the theater in the round
surrounded by summer oaks, cicadas, whippoorwills,
warm breeze drowsy, billowing the cloth of the set,
she sits alone in the first row, shoes off,
loafing and enjoying herself, laughing at
the fool's jokes though the play is a tragedy,
slim, slouching in the comfortable heat then leaning
forward, rapt, chin in hands, elbows on knees
spread wide across the sleeveless light-blue dress
and my throat tightens, knowing it isn't you,
can't possibly be you, but,
not able to make out her features, how
like you used to be she is, and,
abruptly conjured from the trap door of my heart,
from underneath the worn edge of my outrage
at your self-murder twelve years gone,
without warning rises the sharpness of how much,
how much I miss your outrageous laugh,
our youth, the lanky ease of your fierce company.

**Valentine's Day**

You were leaving on the train
as you've done for years
every Monday morning
for a week of work away.

Driving home
from the station, I saw
the ambulance turn, blare
into Milwaukee's empty marina.

Later, I heard,
because it was Valentine's Day
the couple had gone down to the lake
with a camera.

He'd wanted to set her against
the bright copse of city,
so he'd backed out
onto a yellowed floe

thickened by winter. But
the hidden lace of the edge
gave way and he fell, through
to icy water,

innocent of the double
deceit in early spring,
when cracks begin, when what's
seemed solid all along

will soften and leave
nothing, not even the faint
promise of summer, to stand on.
On the news, she told

of the rope that had been
too short, and his last words
—*I can't breathe*--
but most of all, his surprise,

looking out to the far,
unfinished hem
of horizon, then turning
back in bewilderment

toward her, that this was the end,
already, to have come to the end—
incomprehensible--
and then his turning white

right before he was gone.

I know such distances exist
but they never seemed as close,
as non-negotiable as now.
I thought of how, that morning

by the track, we'd kissed,
and tossed our usual goodbyes:
you'd smiled and sketched for me
your familiar sweet salute,

then turned away and slid
behind the glassy, gliding doors
that opened at that moment,
just for you.

## *Theme and Variations*

**Theme and Variations for My Sister**

*theme:*

Soon there will be no one
left
to remember you.

There will be no more
crones
to commune with your bones,

to stitch them together
again, yet
again, with silk thread.

So your bones will
dismember, and the embers
of your life (lived, unlived)

will wash downstream to
the mouth
of the everliving earth.

No Isis will
gather
you in, no one will be

left to mourn except
the wind,
the wind.

*var.1:*

Soon
those who remember you
will also die.

No one
will eat and drink
in remembrance of you,

or wash
your body, or patch
a quilt with your dress.

The grace
of your crippled bones
--legs and hands--

will never
be recalled, nor
fantasies spun for the

long life
you might have lived.
I would gladly be your

Isis,
but am far
from immortal, leaving

the undying wind,
the south wind of Kansas
to chant, chant

enchant your tale.

*var.2:*

Soon Persephone will sink deep
into the dross of earth's
winter

and Demeter will fail to recall
even her grief in the
empty

fields of wheat. In Hades' realm
Persephone will reign,
still

queen of the dead with
no one to breathe her
story.

Splinters of youth, of
even the prospect
of blooms,

will scatter, the demented wind
unable to recount the spring
of its grief.

By the time May parts its buds,
I will be
gone.

*var.3:*

Feverish, so our mother's story goes,
your fingers drummed silent music

onto the pieced quilt.
Both pianist and drummer, you would seek

her estimation of a drum's tone:
was it not beautiful?

I went to the piano to transmute my grief
for a little while

when our father forbade me
to whisper your name.

Everloving sister, I have played
just one

secret song pieced together
from the scraps of your life.

Your fevered rhythm
is mine as well.

Is it not beautiful?

*interlude:*

We overwrite our stories with
the instruments given.

We complicate, rif, play with their fixed
strings, till our elaborate songs emerge,

in distorted cacophony.
Still, in the measured beat beneath

it all, flows the swift current of your name.

*var. 4:*

You were my teacher,
I your Magdalene, your
unsung disciple
who saw your body and said
you were not dead.

The tomb open, you
irreparably gone, my
bones ached. I was
and was not
you.

You ascended to Heaven.

I carefully gathered and stored
your relics.

You were gone in a flash.

I, cracked bell, have
told and told, had time to tell,
to tell,
re-tell.

*var. 5*:

I was the kid sister kicking your crippled leg,
wanting to make sure you were human.

Our mother asked, why couldn't I be more like you?
Revising is not easy: once again scanning the dark

dactyls of your name, rearranging, I wonder,
had you lived, would you have failed her too,

leaving her church and the life she picked out for you?
or would you have signed her contract?

Having a god for a sister is hard.
I am flawed, mortal, old.

This I have learned:
re-versing is not easy.

*return to theme:*

Soon there will be no one
left
to remember you,

> no apostle to stitch together the
> muddled remnants of your story.

My testament remains
your mummy, my only boon
against loss, its sarcophagus
sealed with my name.
.
Swiftly, the current will course
what's left of girl and crone
down to the mouth
of the everdying earth.

> Isis cannot gather us in.
> Nor can she mourn in her windless land.

In life, wind blows.
In life, we expire,
leaving our songs.

Is it not beautiful?

## *About the Author*

Kathleen Dale was born in Kansas, though she has lived on the shore of Lake Michigan for many years, with her husband, Steve Kapelke. They have three grown daughters and two grandsons. She is a serious amateur pianist and has always seen an intimate connection between music and poetry. In June, 2015, she gave her fourth recital of classical music, including works by contemporary American women.

Her blog (**www.kathleenanndale.squarespace.com**) has chronicled her process of preparing the recital as well as of publishing this manuscript.

A Pushcart nominee, Kathleen is also the recipient of several prizes and best-in-issue awards for her poems, which have appeared in over thirty journals. She was nominated for inclusion in *Best American Poetry 2014,* and in Spring, 2013, was featured poet in *The Centrifugal Eye*'s "Sinkhole: Drowning or Surviving—Themes on Coping in Poetic Form."

Proceeds from the sale of this book go to benefit Jazale's Art Studio (*jazalesartstudio.org*), which promotes the arts and education for the youth of Milwaukee.

## Acknowledgements

Thank you to Louisa, Bill, and Judith for their suggestions, as well as to my husband, Steve, for his support.

A few of these poems first appeared in the author's earlier works: *Ties that Bind* (Finishing Line Press, 2006); *Rescue Mission* (Antrim House Press, 2011); and *Avatars of Baubo* (Green Fuse Press, 2013).

Other poems first appeared, sometimes in slightly different form, in the following publications: *The Centrifugal Eye, Chicago Literari, Free Verse, Futurecycle Press, Great Lakes Review, Literary Mama, The Lyric, Persimmon Tree, Poems for Malala, Trillium Review, Verse Wisconsin, Wisconsin People & Ideas, Wisconsin Poets' Calendar.*